Designed by Stuart M. Goldstein

First published in the USA 1980
St. Martin's Press, Inc.,
175 Fifth Avenue
New York, N.Y. 10010

Library of Congress Catalog Card Number
77-74665

Tress, Arthur
    Tress.

    1. Men—United States—Pictorial Works.
2. Masculinity (Psychology)   I. Title.
HQ1090.3.T73   305 3'0973   79-48010
ISBN 0-312-81776-2

Printed in Switzerland by Roto-Sadag, Geneva

For Robert R.

ARTHUR TRESS

Arthur Tress

FACING UP

BERNARD LETU EDITEUR

ST. MARTIN'S PRESS, NEW YORK

New York City n'est ni trash ni beautiful. Pas besoin de porter des badges, de faire campagne pour soutenir l'une ou l'autre cause. New York City est trash et beautiful : c'est une ville terriblement humaine, capable, tout de front, d'insoutenables douceurs quand elle se donne des airs de provinciale et de fascinantes violences quand elle joue son rôle de métropole. New York City est née, là, rivée au roc, d'un hasard fou, rêve d'un siècle. C'est peut-être la seule ville du monde où tous les habitants sont venus d'ailleurs et y vivent, sans jamais oublier l'ailleurs de leur vie. A New York City, on ne peut pas se faire de racines, tout est de hasard et de roc. On passe. On traîne. On se heurte. New York City est toujours en érection. Au-dessus de la ville, dans le ciel, il y a un grand trou. Le ciel de New York City est pur comme nulle autre part. C'est peut-être pour ça que tout le monde vient d'ailleurs. New York City met à nu ceux qui restent dans ses pierres, au hasard des lieux et des rencontres.

Voici Tress, prénom Arthur, guetteur, voyeur, truqueur, croqueur, adorateur de sa ville et de sa vie, gardien de ses propres rêves, maniaque, obsédé, tourmenté, serein quand l'image qu'il crée est très exactement l'image qui le devance dans cette ville, moqueur si on le juge, jamais là quand on lui parle. Tress est le plus grand étourdi de sa ville. Rien ne l'intéresse que cette élection-érection là. Tout ce qui traîne est à lui. Il est tombé dans la caisse à outils des rêves sensuels, des solitudes corporelles, d'un entre-deux-âges, où le face à face, partie à trois, donne tour à tour le droit de jouir, à la ville, à l'autre ou à soi-même. Mais il n'y a jamais de couple véritable. Les jouissances sont toujours solitaires, cruelles parce qu'à cru, dans le sens où l'on monte à cru un cheval pour s'enfuir, rebelle, sous le nez des juges et justiciers.

Il y a une mythologie de New York City dont notre siècle doit tenir compte et dont quelques fous rendent compte au risque des malentendus et des malécoutés. Or, qui dit mythologie, sous-entend imaginaire, fiction délibérée, création qui se prétend pure. Or l'imaginaire de New York City est tout entier, réel, réaliste, dans la pierre, le fer, la ferraille, le somptueux ou le famélique, l'attirail, le décrépi ou le charmant. Tout, sauf le pittoresque. Y voir du pittoresque, c'est ne pas vouloir regarder, aimer cette ville qui a la folie d'être verticale et qui a eu l'audace de faire un trou dans le ciel, donnant le vertige à tous ceux qui y passent, à tous ceux qui y vivent. Les photos de Tress ont ceci de flagrant, flagrant délit, et de fort, qu'il ne faut pas les lire comme des exploits, un spectacle, mais bien comme des constats, une empoignade, passage de quelqu'un qui ne veut pas revenir ailleurs, et qui se perd dedans, dedans la ville, dedans cette ville. Je connais Arthur Tress: je ne le connais pas du tout. Il est dedans. Dans la photo qu'il n'a pas encore faite. Je connais son adresse par cœur, Riverside Drive, c'est tout près des docks. Des docks désaffectés: il n'y a plus de départ. Je crois qu'il ira jusqu'au bout de son histoire, quelques rouleaux-photo, vierges, dans la tête.

Yves Navarre

New York is neither trashy nor beautiful. No need to wear buttons and campaign for one view or the other. New York is both trashy and beautiful. It's a terribly human city, at once capable of unbearable gentleness when it acts like a village and fascinating violence when it plays the metropolis. Dream of an age, New York was born, riveted to rock, by some mad chance. It's probably the only city in the world whose inhabitants all come from some-where else and live there without ever forgetting the somewhere else of their lives. You can't put down roots in New York. Everything is chance and rock. You pass through it, hang around it, bump against it. New York is constantly in erection. In the sky above the city there's a big hole. New York's sky is the purest anywhere. Maybe that's why everyone comes from somewhere else. New York strips naked those who stay among its stones, caught in unexpected places and chance encounters.

Here's Tress, first name Arthur, prowler, voyeur, trickster, devourer, lover of his city and its life, keeper of his own dreams. An obsessed, tormented, maniacal man, he calms down only when the image he captures is exactly the image which lured him in this city. Mocking when you judge him, never there when you speak to him, Tress is the greatest day-dreamer in town. Nothing interests him but his own obsessions. Everything left lying around belongs to him. He has fallen into the toolbox of sensual dreams and bodily solitudes of some indeterminate age, where a face to face encounter becomes a threesome that gives each in turn the right to come – the city, the other, oneself. For real couples don't exist. Coming is always a solitary act, and cruel because it's bare,

in the sense of mounting bareback on a horse in order to flee, rebelliously, under the very noses of judges and lawmen.

There's a mythology of New York that our times must take into account, and that some madmen do account for at the risk of being misunderstood and misinterpreted. Now mythology implies something imaginary, a deliberate fiction, a supposedly pure creation. But New York's mythology is solid, real, realistic; it's in stone, steel, and scrap, in the sumptuous and the starved, in broken down and fascinating machinery. It's everything except picturesque. To find New York picturesque is to refuse to look at or to love this city, which is mad enough to be vertical and audacious enough to make a hole in the sky, causing dizziness in all who pass through or live there. Tress's photos are forceful, flagrant, and in flagrante delicto because they are not to be read as exploits or as a spectacle, but as statements, the grip and mark of someone who won't return to somewhere else, and who gets lost inside, inside the city, inside this city. I know Arthur Tress. I don't know him at all. He's inside. Inside the photo he hasn't taken yet. I know his adress by heart – Riverside Drive. It's right near the docks, the abandoned docks, where there are no more departures. I think he'll go to the very end of his life with a few rolls of film, unused, inside his head.

Yves Navarre

(translated by George Stambolian)

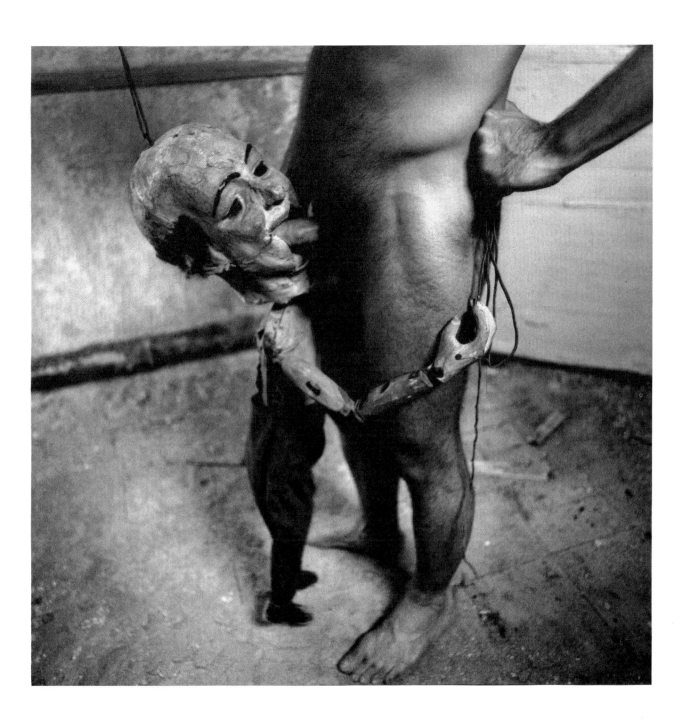

BIBLIOGRAPHIE

Songs of the Blue Ridge Mountains
        Oak Press, New York, 1968

Open Space and the Inner City
        New York State Council on the Arts, 1970

The Dream Collector
        Westover, Richmond, Va., 1972
        Avon Books, New York, 1973

Shadow
        Avon Books, New York, 1975

Theater of the Mind
        Morgan and Morgan, New York, 1976

Rêves
        Editions Complexe, Bruxelles, 1979

photo by Duane Michals

BIOGRAPHIE

1940   Naissance à Brooklyn, New York, le 24 Novembre.

1962   Diplôme du Bard College, New York (Beaux-Arts).

1963-66   Voyages au Mexique, Japon, Inde et Europe consacrés à l'étude de l'Histoire de l'Art et des cultures anciennes.

1967-68   Photographe ethnographe – travaux sur plusieurs groupes tribaux: Mayas, Dogons, Eskimos et Lapons.

1969-70   Photographe documentaliste au service d'Agences gouvernementales américaines pour la préparation d'études sur des groupes ethniques défavorisés.

1972-76   Se sent attiré par le surréalisme en photographie et sa révélation de l'irrationnel. Subit l'influence des écrits de Jung et d'Eliade. Publie des ouvrages sur les rêves d'enfants, sur certaines visions mystiques personnelles et sur l'univers mental et privé des adultes.

1977-79   Conçoit le projet d'un livre sur les fantasmes de l'érotisme homosexuel masculin centré sur le phallus comme source d'imagerie.

Vit actuellement à New York City.

BIOGRAPHY

1940   Born Brooklyn, New York.

1962   Bachelor of Fine Arts, Bard College, N.Y.

1963-66   Travels in Mexico, Japan, India, and Europe studying Art History and ancient cultures.

1967-68   Works as ethnographic photographer recording several primitive tribal groups: Mayans, Dogons, Eskimo, Lapps.

1969-70   Works as documentary photographer for U.S. Government Agencies preparing studies of ethnic poverty groups.

1972-76   Becomes interested in Surrealistic photography and its attempt to reveal the hidden sphere of the Irrational. Is influenced by the writings of Jung and Eliade. Publishes books on the dreams of children, personal mystic visions, and the private mental world of adults.

1977-79   Does project on male erotic fantasy centering around the phallus as source of imagery.

Lives in New York City.